PET JOKES
THAT WiLL
MAKE YOU HOWL!

Terry Pierce and Ruth Musgrave
Illustrated by Laura Coyle

STERLING

New York / London
www.sterlingpublishing.com/kids

To my inspiration for this book—Orca, BJ and Rin—and the people who supported me in writing it—Mark, Greg, Mailea, my parents, Cecilia and Ruth.

Terry Pierce

To those who gave me the gift of laughter: my parents, Ampy, Ayslinn, Terry, and my best friends Indy, Sam, Bailey, Jake, and Max.

Ruth Musgrave

Design by Lucy Wilner

STERLING and the distinctive Sterling logo are registered trademarks of Sterling Publishing Co., Inc.

Library of Congress Cataloging-in-Publication Data
Pierce, Terry.
    Pet jokes that will make you howl! / Terry Pierce & Ruth Musgrave
    ; illustrated by Laura Coyle.
        p. cm.
    Includes index.
    ISBN 1-4027-1904-3
    1. Pets—Humor.   I. Musgrave, Ruth, 1960-   . II. Title.
PN6231.P42P54 2005
818'.60208—dc22

2005021664

10 9 8 7 6 5 4 3 2 1

Published by Sterling Publishing Co., Inc.
387 Park Avenue South, New York, NY 10016
© 2005 by Terry Pierce and Ruth Musgrave
Distributed in Canada by Sterling Publishing
c/o Canadian Manda Group, 165 Dufferin Street
Toronto, Ontario, Canada M6K 3H6
Distributed in the United Kingdom by GMC Distribution Services
Castle Place, 166 High Street, Lewes, East Sussex, England BN7 1XU
Distributed in Australia by Capricorn Link (Australia) Pty. Ltd.
P.O. Box 704, Windsor, NSW 2756, Australia

Manufactured in the United States of America
All rights reserved

Sterling ISBN-13: 978-1-4027-1904-2 Hardcover
        ISBN-10: 1-4027-1904-3

        ISBN-13: 978-1-4027-4839-4 Paperback
        ISBN-10: 1-4027-4839-6

For information about custom editions, special sales, premium and corporate purchases, please contact Sterling Special Sales Department at 800-805-5489 or specialsales@sterlingpub.com.

Contents

1 Double Dog Dare You to Laugh

Playing Favorites

What's a dog's favorite kind of pizza?
Pupperoni.

What's a dog's favorite sci-fi show?
Bark Trek.

What's a dog's favorite festival?
Mardi paw.

What's a dog's favorite frozen treat?
Pupsicles.

What's a dog's favorite candy?
A lolli-pup.

What's a puppy's favorite game?
Peek-a-bow-wow.

Double Crossings

What do you get when you cross a dog and a car?
A dog that chases its taillights.

What do you get when you cross a dog and a goose?
A dog that honks at cars instead of chasing them.

What do you get when you cross a dog and a rug?
A dog that lies around all the time.

What do you get when you cross a dog and jalapeno pepper?
A chili dog.

Grrrrrrr!

How can you recognize a bird dog?
It has feathers.

Did you hear about the giant dog that attacks cities?
Its name is Dogzilla.

Which city is run by dogs?
  Chidoggo.

Why did the dog throw the watch away?
  She didn't like ticks.

Where do dogs hate to shop?
  A flea market.

What did the puppy call his grouchy grandfather?
  Grrrrrand-paw.

VETERINARIAN: Your dog is mean inside and out.
DOG OWNER: How can you tell?
VETERINARIAN: Even his stomach is growling.

Follow the Bouncing Ball

What's the favorite toy of a dog with no teeth?
A gumball.

What's the favorite ball of a goofy dog?
An oddball.

What is a hungry dog's favorite ball?
A meatball.

What is an arcade dog's favorite ball?
A pinball.

What's the favorite ball of a silly dog?
A screwball.

TEACHER: Spot, where's your chewed-up homework?
SPOT: I swiped little Johnny's spelling list, but he took
   the words right out of my mouth.

DAVE: My dog brings in a lot of money.
ANNA: Oh! Is he a show dog?
DAVE: No, a pickpocket.

ROSS: Did you hear about the mummified dog they
   found in a pyramid?
HOSS: No, who was it?
ROSS: King Pup.

MAX: Can you order us lunch?
JAKE: Sure. Here kitty kitty.

HOSS: Did you hear they just found King Pup's
    girlfriend in the tomb next door?
ROSS: No. Who was she?
HOSS: Nef-furr-titi.

REX: ...and here's a picture of a piece of greasy bread.
    Here's a photo of the pork chop I got after
    Thursday's dinner...
DIGGER: What is this book?
REX: It's my scrap book.

FIDO: I saw the ugliest cat on TV last night.
SPOT: Really? What did you do?
FIDO: I knocked him right off the set.

Spot: Why was your grandma tossed out of the "Yappy Home" dance recital?
PRINCESS: I guess you can't teach an old dog new kicks.

BLOSSOM: Did you hear about the dog that started a business retrieving lost sand art?
MAGGIE: No, what's it called?
BLOSSOM: Fetch-a-sketch.

Woof, Woof... Who's there?

Woof, woof.
  Who's there?
Anita.
  Anita who?
Anita bone.

Woof, woof.
  Who's there?
Alfredo.
  Alfredo who?
Alfredo the vet.

Woof, woof.
  Who's there?
Apple.
  Apple who?
Apple your tail if you do that again.

Woof, woof.
  Who's there?
Canoe.
  Canoe who?
Canoe stop pulling my tail?

Woof, woof.
　Who's there?
Catsup.
　Catsup who?
Catsup up the tree,
'cause the dog chased
him.

Woof, woof.
　Who's there?
Dogma.
　Dogma who?
Dogma says I can't go
out to play.

Woof, woof.
　Who's there?
Doggone.
　Doggone who?
Dog gone home, cat's
in charge.

Woof, woof.
　Who's there?
Dogwood.
　Dogwood who?
Dogwood if he could,
but he can't.

HOWL ABOUT A LiTTLE TUNE

When Saint Bernards Go Marching In

Frisky the Snow Dog

Yankee Poodle

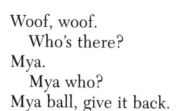

Woof, woof.
  Who's there?
Mya.
  Mya who?
Mya ball, give it back.

> Woof, woof.
>   Who's there?
> Sawyer.
>   Sawyer who?
> Sawyer cat. Let's run!

Woof, woof.
  Who's there?
Sticker.
  Sticker who?
Sticker round, it's treat time.

> Woof, woof.
>   Who's there?
> Ulysses.
>   Ulysses who?
> Ulysses the squirrel, then chases it.

My doghouse is sooo small...

I don't have room to change my mind.
The fleas moved out.
There's no room to shed.
I keep poking myself in the eye with my tail.

4-PAWS-UP MOViES

Lord of the Springers: The Two Bow-wowers

Indiana Bones and the Temple of Food

Poodles of the Caribbean

Mary Puppins

Dogula

Perfect Choice

A woman goes to an animal shelter to adopt a dog. Only two are available. One, a delicate golden-haired dog rests quietly inside his neat-as-a-pin doghouse. The second, a large and tough-looking dog, is sitting on top of what's left of a demolished doghouse. It's been shattered by the dog's weight and splintered by its teeth. Pointing to the bulky dog, the woman says, "I'll take that one!"

The animal shelter worker can't believe his ears. "Why, in heaven's name, would you take that dog?"

"Because," she explained patiently, "he's already housebroken.

PAW THROUGH THESE BOOKS

Trashy Treats by Tippy Cann

It's a Full Moon by C. Spot Howel

Impulse Control by Ada Katt

Those Awful Hunting Dogs! by Frieda Squirrel

Scaredy Cats by T. Zingdawg

New Leash on Life by Ben Shoppin

My Human, My Best Friend by R. Dawg

Puppy Loves

MARIA: My dog loves to go to the library.
SHARON: So what's the problem?
MARIA: He can't read.

GEORGE: My dog loves to beat me to the newspaper.
MARIA: So what's the problem?
GEORGE: He shreds.

JAMIE: My dog loves to sleep on the bed.
MARTIN: So what's the problem?
JAMIE: He makes me sleep on the floor.

FRAN: My dog loves to eat from my hand.
MAX: So what's the problem?
FRAN: He eats all my sandwiches."

CANiNE LiCENSE PLATES

FLYNFR

K9ZRUL

LNGWK

UNLSHD

TLWGNTM

DGTRTS

KTZSTNK

CATS STINK
DOG TREATS
TAIL WAGGIN' TIME
UNLEASHED
LONG WALK
CANINES RULE
FLYIN' FUR

LICENSE PLATES UNLOCKED

2 Who Let the Dog Jokes Out?

What do you call young dogs playing in wet snow?
Slush puppies.

What do you call a sweet bubbly pooch?
A soda pup.

What do you call a sour pooch?
A pup tart.

Where do lucky dogs sit during the baseball game?
In the dog-out.

What's it called when a dog hits a baseball high into the air?
A pup fly.

Why did the car quit rolling after the puppy changed the tires?
It was dog tired.

Why did the dog cross the road?
To get to the cat on the other side.

Why couldn't the dog do the foxtrot?
Because it's a dog.

Why can't dogs dance?
They have two left feet.

Why did the dog go to a vocal coach for howling lessons?
She wanted to be a pup star.

What's a dog's favorite kind of chicken?
Bark-be-que.

What's a dog's favorite napping chair?
A bark-a-lounger.

Where do young dogs sleep when they go camping?
In pup tents.

What do you call a dog psychic?
  A paw reader.

What did the star-struck puppy request from the
famous dog?
  A paw-tograph.

Where do you store a puppy's food?
  In pupperware.

Why was the young dog always surrounded by
friends?
  He was pupular.

Why was the dog barking up the wrong tree?
He needed glasses.

Why did the impatient dog need to see a dog
psychiatrist?
He had a wait problem.

I See (Not!)

Barney had a beautiful coat of thick fur and no
problem with fleas. His friend Earl, on the other hand,
had a very thin coat and felt like he was crawling with
them. Barney helped Earl search his fur, but they
didn't see any fleas. So Barney took Earl to see a vet.
After the exam, the vet said, "I know why you can't see
any fleas. "Why?" the two pals asked. The vet
answered, "Because these fleas vanish into thin hair."

MORE 4-PAWS-UP MOVIES

Kitty Kitty Bang Bang

Beauty and the Beagle

Little Furr-maid

Home Work

How many dogs does it take to clean the house?
One dog and a fluffy cat to reach the hard places.

Why did the dog clean all day?
He wanted to take a bite out of grime.

Why did the dog use a toy to clean the house?
He wanted it squeaky clean.

VETERINARIAN: I have some bad news for you. You have fleas.
SPOT: I want a second opinion.
VETERINARIAN: Okay. You're lousy at playing fetch!

FLUFFY: What do you call a slow squirrel?
REX: Lunch.

KING: I hate the dog park.
PRINCE: WHY?
KING: It's such a flea-for-all.

More Puppy Loves

PAUL: My dog loves to chase the ball.
DAVID: So what's the problem?
PAUL: It bothers the basketball team.

EDIE: My dog loves to get the newspaper.
TAMMY: So what's the problem?
EDIE: The neighbors haven't read it yet.

SALLY: My dog loves fresh eggs in the morning.
ANDY: That's great.
SALLY: The neighbor's chickens don't think so.

Bowser's Bath

What did the dog say to the lousy groomer?
You rub me the wrong way.

Why did the groomer throw dog hair into the fan?
She wanted to see the fur fly.

Did you hear about the groomer who had to work on Halloween?
It's a hairy tale.

What's it called when a dog gets her nails done?
A paw-dicure.

PRINCESS: I don't like that new groomer.
PEARL: Why?
PRINCESS: She's snippy.

GROOMER: I refuse to groom your dirty and mean poodle.
OWNER: Why?
GROOMER: He's too snarlie.

FIFI: I really like this new groomer. He's very funny.
FLUFFY: Yeah, he's a real cut-up.

SAM: My dog just stormed out of the groomers.
VICKI: Why?
SAM: He was ticked off.

Time for School

What did the teacher complain about when she had too many puppies in a class?
Over-pupulation.

DOG TRAINER (shouting across the room): "Your dog is spoiled."
OWNER (shouting back) "How can you tell? You haven't met him yet."
DOG TRAINER: "I can smell him from here."

RUSTY: Hey, did you hear? I got accepted to dog college?
ROXIE: No, how?
RUSTY: I passed my S.I.T.s.

BUSTER: Uh-oh, I'm late for class.
SPOT: Which one?
BUSTER: The Art of Bones
SPOT: Who teaches that?
BUSTER: Mr. Chew.

More Woof Woofs

Woof, woof.
  Who's there?
Icon.
  Icon who?
Icon hop that fence, can you?

Woof, woof.
  Who's there?
Isaiah.
  Isaiah who?
Isaiah, "Woof," weren't you
listening?

Woof, woof.
  Who's there?
Treatment.
  Treatment who?
Treatment for me?

Woof, woof.
  Who's there?
Untidy.
  Untidy who?
Untidy dog, his leash is caught.

DOG-EARED BOOKS

Kissed a Bumper by Chevy Chaser

How to Train Your Owner by Imin Charge

Sneaking Out by Doug Holes

Found Hound by Ben Lost

Fat Cat by E.Z. Tocatch

in The News

By Bow-wow Walters

Hairy's Next Adventure: Interview with J.K. Growling
Dog Chases Car and Catches It
Dog Trains Owner to Sleep on Floor

DOG-TiONARY

Lap: Something to sleep on.

Table: Something to climb on.

Come here: Only has meaning when a treat or toy are present.

Mine: Includes anything a dog wants to sit on, sleep on, chew, play with or eat.

No: [Not in the dictionary]

KRISTA: What are you doing?
ERICA: Looking for my dog.
KRISTA: Where did you leave her?
ERICA: In the barking lot.

Good Relations!

Every day two little puppies, Spot and Prince, played at the park. For three days in a row, a much larger and stronger dog would join them. But he played too rough, made Prince cry, and took their snacks.

Finally one night, Spot told his father about the bully. The next day, Spot and Prince's fathers waited and watched with their pups. When the bully started to play rough, the fathers moved in and grabbed the dog by the scruff of his neck.

The startled dog yelped, and howled at the puppies, "Hey, get your Pa's off of me."

3 Pugs & Kisses

What do you call a dog who thinks he's smarter than others?

A smug pug.

What did the hungry bird dog ask the hunter?

Did you bring cheese to go with these quackers?

What do you call a dog that lives between two countries?

A border collie.

What dog do new parents need?
A bassinet hound.

What dog do you get when you cross a stinging insect and an ocean bird?
A beegull.

What do you call a royal hunting dog?
Regal beagle.

What does a regal beagle become when she becomes queen?
A crowned hound.

Why are bloodhounds such good reporters?
They have a nose for news.

What is a dog's favorite part of the train?
The boxer cars.

What do you get when you cross a bird and a bird dog?
A cockatiel spaniel.

What do you get when you cross Lassie with a rose?
Collie-flower.

Why did the doberman destroy the clock?
He was killing time.

What kind of dog helps Santa?
An elf hound.

What do giant sequoias and German shepherd dogs have in common?
Both have a lot of bark.

What is the fastest way for a dog to travel?
Greyhound bus.

How can you tell when a herding dog is embarrassed?
He looks sheepish.

What is a sled dog's favorite meal?
Mush.

What's it called when a pit bull trips?
A pit fall.

What do you call a pit bull without a hind end?
A bottomless pit.

What giant dog is made of strawberry, vanilla and chocolate ice cream?
A Neapolitan mastiff.

What dog does a teacher use to teach geography?
A pointer.

What do you call a psychic that reads small furry dogs?
A palm-oranian reader.

Did you hear about the dog that had pasta for fur?
It's a noodle-poodle.

What do you call a spoiled dog?
A rottenweiler.

What do schnauzers eat for breakfast?
Schnausages.

CUSTOMER: Waiter, waiter! There's something furry in my drink!
WAITER: Of course, sir. It's a tea-cup poodle.

CUSTOMER: Waiter, waiter! What's this tiny poodle doing in my tea?
WAITER: The dog paddle, sir!

What do you get when you cross a poodle and a potato?

Curly fries.

How can you tell when a wiener dog is hungry?

It eats with relish.

What's a little dog's favorite newspaper for house training?

Yorkie Times.

FIDO: I sent twenty beagles to Spot to remind him to pay his bill.
SPIKE: Why beagles?
FIDO: That guy really needed to be hounded.

DONNA: I'm so mad. I just took my dog to the worst groomer.
KRISTA: What makes you say that? I think your poodle *looks gorgeous!*
DONNA: It's a bulldog.

TEACUP POODLE: Why do you call me "Conardly"?
GREAT DANE: 'Cause you're so small I conardly see you.

These Hit the Spot

What's it called when someone jabs a Dalmatian?
Poke a dot.

Why did the super-clean Dalmatian bleach his fur?
He wanted everything to be spotless.

Firehouse best-seller:
Polka Do or Polka Don't? by Dal Mation

Not So Puzzling

Every morning, Betty and Ross ate breakfast at an outdoor cafe. One morning, a man with five Dalmatians on the leash approached the coffee shop. Stopping, he pulled each dog to him and hooked the spotted dogs' leashes together one by one. Finally, he tied the last leash to a nearby tree. "That's strange," Ross said. "What's he doing?"
    Betty said, "Isn't it obvious? He's connecting the dots."

What's it called when you kiss a dog?
A pooch smooch.

What do you call a lost dog that comes home?
A found hound.

What happens to a dog that eats too many donuts?
It becomes a round hound.

Hot Diggity Dog

NANCY: What do you put on a chili dog?
PAUL: A sweater.

What kind of dog can be hot and cold?
A chilly chili dog.

MORE CANINE LiCENSE PLATES

KTCHSR

DGBRETH

4PWDRV

BNZRGR8

BONES 'R GREAT.
4 PAW DRIVE
DOG BREATH
CAT CHASER

LICENSE PLATES UNLOCKED

DOGISMS

#21: Expensive shoes taste better.
#34: Under the bed is the best place
     to hide things.
#55: Sticks and bones...make a dog very happy.
#99: All play and no work...make you a dog.

Why do dogs have fur?
Scales would look funny.

What do you get when you cross a dog with a cat?
A dog that ignores you.

JEFF: I think I know how my robotic pet dog got a virus.
JANE: How?
JEFF: It got a bad byte.

What kind of dog can translate when a dog wants to talk to a duck?
A bird dog.

My water bowl is sooo big...
    I can dog paddle in it.
    I think I saw a shark's fin.
    You can't find Nemo in it.
    If I bump it, dolphins can surf the wave.

4 Sticks and Bones

What are a sea dog's favorite sticks?
Fish sticks.

What is a neat dog's favorite game?
Pick-up sticks.

What is a goofy dog's favorite stick?
Slapstick.

What's the favorite stick of a dog model?
  Lipstick.

What are twin dogs' favorite sticks?
  Matchsticks.

What's the favorite stick of a wizard's dog?
  A broomstick.

What's the favorite stick of a dog that's afraid of the dark?
  Candlestick.

What's the favorite stick of a dog that's always slipping and sliding?
  Nonstick.

What are the favorite sticks of a dog who likes a hard beat?
  Drumsticks.

Bad-to-the-Bone Jokes

Who is a dog's favorite historical figure?
  Napoleon Bonaparte.

What's a dog's favorite rock band?
  The Rolling Bones.

Who is a dog's favorite spy?
  Bones. James Bones.

What did the surfer dog say when he saw the bone?
Gnawsome!

Did you hear, they found the skeleton of an ancient explorer in Indianapolis?
Oh, you mean Indiana Bones?

A Dog By Any Other Name... Still Smells Like a Dog

What do you call a dog that breaks through doors?
Buster.

What is a poodle's natural nickname?
Curly.

What do you call an archeologist's dog?
Digger.

What do you call a dog with only two legs?
Eileen.

What do you call a dog that's always getting stepped on?
Matt.

What do you call a dog that only eats food tossed from the table?
Scrappy.

What do you call a dog that destroys everything?
Rex.

What do get when you cross a hot beverage with the king of dogs?

Tea-Rex.

What is a dog made of glass called?

Py-Rex.

What is the new name of the former movie star dog who gained a lot of weight?

Rin-ton-ton.

What do you call a dog that wanders off?

Rover.

What do you call the firefighter's dog?
Sparky.

What do you call a dog that's one solid color?
Spot.

What do you call the lawyer's dog?
Sue.

What do you call the magician's dog?
Trixie.

What was the dog's junkyard called?
Rex's Wrecks.

DOG-EARED BOOKS

Scratchy Tales by Iva Flea

Caught in the Rain by Soggy Doggy

Why Dogs Rule by Kay Nine

Hole in the Fence by Seymour Dawgs

I've Gotta Go by Anita Tree

MORE DOGISMS

#22: Whatever side of the couch you're on…is mine.

#73: It's a dog eat dog food world.

#115: When you're the dog walker, the view never changes.

5 Doggone Wildlife

Where do wolves go to become stars?
  Howliewood.

Why wouldn't the veterinarian operate on the
laughing hyena?
  He was already in stitches.

Fox: That hyena is so annoying.
WOLF: Why?
FOX: He always has to have the last laugh.

Why are wolves great movers?
They love to pack.

What's a wolf's favorite fast food?
Squirrels.

What's a wolf's favorite holiday?
Howl o'ween.

COYOTE: Waiter, there's a hare in my soup.
WAITER: Well, you did order rabbit stew!

What do you get when you cross a wolf and a chimp?
A howler monkey.

What's a wolf's favorite way to fly?
In a howlie-copter.

What do you get when you cross a rattlesnake with a
fox who gossips?
A rattle tattle tail.

TEACHER: How can you tell the difference between a
    dog and a wolf?
STUDENT: They're spelled differently.

Why did the man regret letting the tiny shiny fish
pack for his vacation?
They packed like sardines.

What's a toad's favorite part of the newspaper?
The wart ads.

Why did the man put the trout on a plane?
He wanted to see flying fish.

How does a camel hide in the desert?
Camel-flage

What do you get when you cross a frog and another pocket pet?
Green legs and hamster.

FREDDIE: How about teaching your pet rabbit to balance on his head?
ROBERT: What for?
FREDDIE: That way your hare can stand on end.

HERMAN: Ollie Owl used to be popular and talked up a storm. Now he's always alone.
HARMON: Yes, too bad. These days his friends say he doesn't give a hoot.

What do you call a fat parrot?
Roly Polly

Why did the bat's surgery practice fail?
It was a fly-by-night operation.

What keeps food dangerously cold?
A refriger-gator

Hiss-terical Humor

What's a snake's favorite subject in school?
Hiss-tory

Why did the garter snake and king cobra spit at each other when they met?
They were hissing cousins.

What do you call a single slithering reptile?
A Miss Snake.

Why did the cobra hiss at his reflection in the mirror?
It was his spitting image.

A cobra ended his phone call with a violent hiss.
"Who was that?" his friend asked
The cobra responded, "Sorry, I never hiss and tell."

Every day, the gym teacher quacked out orders.
Count off in twos. In turn, each duckling said their
number, "Two, four, six…and so on." One day a
student asked, "Why do we always count in even
numbers?" The teacher said, "I don't like odd ducks."

Watered-down Humor

Why was the hermit crab frustrated?
It was shell bound.

What did the walrus say after the seal kissed him?
Yuck! My lips are sealed!

What do you call female seahorses that only come out in the dark?
Night mares.

Duck! incoming Jokes

A pigeon was hanging out near the pond. All day long the ducks quacked and squawked about this great movie at the drive-in. That night, the pigeon decided to see what the fuss was about. The next day, one of the ducks asked him what he thought of the movie.

The pigeon shrugged, saying "I didn't think it was all it was quacked up to be."

MANUEL: Did you hear? Some people are trying to save a poor water bird that's trapped between some fallen rocks and the side of a cliff!
JOSE: Say again, but make it short.
MANUEL: Duck stuck between a rock and a hard place.

Something Fishy

What's the goofiest fish in the sea?
The clownfish.

What did one shark say to the other after eating some clownfish?
Did that fish taste funny to you?

What do you get when you cross a fish and a basketball player?
Shark-ille O'Neill

Out Behind the Barn

ED: Never go to a horse for change.
ALICE: Why not?
ED: They only use horse cents.

Where does a young cow eat?
It the calf-eteria.

What kind of karate moves do sheep use?
Lamb chops.

SCRATCH AND SNiFF TiTLES

Stripes: A Fashion Don't by Leo Pard
Spots: The Real Fashion Don't by Tye Garr

Untamed Humor

What's a rodent's favorite carnival ride?
  A ferret's wheel.

What scampers through houses stealing teeth from under the pillows?
  The tooth ferret.

What do you call a pocket pet that talks too much?
  A verbal gerbil.

What do you call a fat bird?
  A pudgy budgie.

TEXT MESSAGING

Duck #1: L8r G8r
Bunny #2: U hv 2 go?
Duck #1: No. I C a G8r

Eagle #1: Y R U so F@?
Eagle #2: I 8 a C@, a R@, and a B@

BOOKS FLYING OFF THE SHELF

Look Out Below by P. Jahn

Bird Watching by I. Segal

Living the Big Life by E. Norm Mouse

Uninvited Guests

Johnny's mom said "No" to an ant farm, but one day Johnny bought one and brought it home. Suddenly he heard her car in the driveway. When he tried to hide the ant farm, it fell and broke open! Johnny quickly swept up the ants, sand, and glass, dumping everything into a big flowerpot in his room. And that's how Johnny got ants in his plants!

6 A-mewsing Antics

What do good little kittens get at the doctor's office?
Scratch 'n sniff stickers.

What's the first thing shoppers do when they get
home from the pet store?
They let the cat out of the bag.

What do you call a cat who plays the trumpet?
Puss n' toots.

Where do cats invest their money?
In the stalk market.

What state has the most cats?
Catifornia.

How does secret cat agent 007 like his cream?
Shaken, not purred.

What do you get when you cross a feline with a metal detector?
A cat scan.

What's yellow, has four wheels and meows?
A taxi cat.

What do kittens send Santa every year?
A cata-list.

What's it called when a feline basketball star misses the hoop?
A hair ball.

What's it called when a cat walks directly from one place to another?
A feline beeline.

What kind of stories do cats like?
Hairy tales.

Where do Halloween cats go to school?
The Academy of Fine Arches.

What was the Cheshire cat's motto?
There's more than one way to grin a cat.

Cat Math

If a train leaves Kansas City at 4:00 AM and travels 70 miles per hour with Max the cat in the caboose, and another train leaves Chicago at 7:00 AM and travels 85 miles per hour, with Bootsy in the caboose, what time is it when both trains arrive in Denver?
Time to wake up the cats.

GREG: I couldn't get my computer to work last night.
MEG: What was the problem?
GREG: My cat ate the mouse.

Kooky Kitty Knock-Knocks

Knock-knock.
  Who's there?
Acute.
  Acute who?
Acute kitten. Will you
adopt me?

Knock-knock.
  Who's there?
Along.
  Along who?
Along tailed cat in a
room full of rocking
chairs better be careful!

Knock-knock.
  Who's there?
Adjust.
  Adjust who?
Adjust want to curl up
on your lap.

Knock-knock.
  Who's there?
Cattle.
  Cattle who?
Cattle meow when he's
hungry.

Knock-knock.
  Who's there.
Kitten.
  Kitten who?
Kitten you hear me? I've been knocking for five minutes.

Knock-knock.
  Who's there?
Wayne N.
  Wayne N. who?
Wayne N. cats and dogs.

UNSUNG SONGS

"Down in the Alley" by Tom Katz

"Jungle Bells" by A. Jaguar

"Up on the Mousetop" by Carol N. Katz

"Hush, Litter Baby" by C. M. Kitnz

"My Country Hiss of Thee" by Maddy Katz

How did the writer's fat tabby cat get his exercise? *He watched for balls of wadded up paper, then batted around the ideas.*

Whisker Twisters

Cats wipe white wet whiskers with raspy rough tongues.

Tiny Timbuktu tabbies take trips to Toledo.

Manx and minks miss missile missions.

KiTTY SCRATCHES

Cats: The Best Pets by Ima Cat

On the Fence at Midnight by Howell N. Katz

Facial Hair Extensions by Wes Kurz

Adopting Kittens and Puppies by Q.T. Pets

Funny Feline Sayings

When the cat's away, the mice will play…checkers, ping-pong, cards…

It's raining cats and dogs! Don't step in a poodle!

Curiosity killed the cat…that's why cats don't want to go to school.

When the cat's got your tongue, you better not give him any lip.

Dead men tell no tales…and Manx cats have no tails.

Pussycat, Pussycat, where have you been? Out for pizza and ice cream.

You're the cat's pajamas. I guess that makes me the dog's bathrobe.

MARK: Why did you buy your cat a cell phone?
CLARK: So she can make catcalls!

GREG: You look like the cat that swallowed the canary.
PEG: You mean, I look guilty?
GREG: No, you have feathers in your teeth!

PURRRSONALiZED LiCENSE PLATES

NOT4K9S

KTZRULE

YNOTPRR

PRRRFCTN

CATI2D

QTKTN

ILUVCRM

I LOVE CREAM
CUTE KITTEN
CATTITUDE
PURRFECTION
WHY NOT PURR
CATS RULE
NOT FOR CANINES

LICENSE PLATES UNLOCKED

7 Cat's Up Again!

What did medieval cats do for sport?
Mousting.

What do you get when you cross a western bad guy with a cat?
An outclaw.

Where do cats like to sightsee?
The Catacombs.

How many cats does it take to screw in a light bulb?
One. He holds the light bulb while the rest of the world revolves around him.

What do you get when you cross a cat with a fallen tree?
A cat-alog.

Why couldn't the cat finish watching the video?
He kept hitting paws.

What do cats do after a wedding?
They wait for the bride and groom so they can throw mice.

Why aren't cats great golfers?
They're purr for the course.

How do cats label their towels?
Hiss and hers.

Where do cats go to become soldiers?
Military Acat-emy.

What do you call a grouchy cat who doesn't take care of himself?
A crabby shabby tabby.

Make It So

Long ago, a powerful ruler decided that the cats and dogs in his kingdom should live in harmony. To make that happen, he ordered that they all live within his castle walls. Still, people doubted it would work. Felines and canines living in peace? But after a week, they all managed to get along. It was a miracle! Why was the wise king so successful?
He reigned cats and dogs.

MAMA CAT: Knock-knock.
KITTEN: Who's there?
MAMA CAT: Archer.
KITTEN: Archer who?
MAMA CAT: Archer back on Halloween!

RUTH: Did you hear about the seven-toed cat that juggles?
TERRY: No.
RUTH: People are amazed at his feat!

BOSSY: Did you hear about the cream shortage?
OREO: It's a cat-astrophe!

Kooky Kitty Knock-Knocks

Knock-knock.
   Who's there?
Avette.
   Avette who?
Avette made a house call
when my cat was sick.

Knock-knock.
   Who's there?
Claude.
   Claude who?
Claude his way up a tree and now my cat's stuck.

Knock-knock.
   Who's there?
F. Violet.
   F. Violet who?
F. Violet the cat out, will you let it back in?

Knock-knock.
  Who's there?
Seema.
  Seema who?
Seema cat?
I just adopted him!

Knock-knock.
  Who's there?
Wes knew.
  Wes knew who?
Wes knew, pussycat?

Wrong Answer

One morning, a clergyman found a box outside his door. When he opened it, he saw nine newborn kittens. He slapped his forehead, looked up, and said, "I prayed for new pews, not mews!"

Dorky Definitions

Bobcat: A Halloween game played by dogs.

Catwalk: What cats in Asia cook with.

Catacomb: A feline grooming tool.

Cataract: Where cats hang their coats.

Caterpillar: What Bootsy rests his head on.

Catkin: A cat's aunt and uncle.

Catnapping: A kitten abduction.

Catsup: Where the cat goes when the dog chases him.

Cattails: What kittens like hearing at bedtime.

Catty-corner: Where naughty kittens have to sit.

Cat's Eye: A yes vote at a cat meeting.

Cheetah: A cat who looks at another cat's test.

Hairball: When a cat throws up to the basketball hoop—and misses.

Meerkat: A cat with a reflective personality.

CAT HEADLINES

Cat Burglar Collared by Police

Cat Show Winner Claws Its Way to Top

Cat Show Loser Throws Hissy-Fit

Missing Lynx Found: Origin of Cats Explained

Manx Cat Survives Fire But Has No Tale To Tell

Why can't cats fly airplanes?
They always go into a tail spin.

What's a cat's favorite cereal?
Mice Krispies.

How does a cat sign a letter?
Hugs and hisses.

What's a cat's favorite dessert?
Mice cream.

What state has the angriest cats?
Hiss-issippi.

What state has the most kittens?
Mew York.

What is a kitten's favorite toy?
A Mew-Master.

What does a kitten call its parents?
Ma and Paw.

Where do cats keep their art supplies?
In the glitter box.

How do cats start playing a board game?
They roll the mice.

How does a kitten know when his mother means business?
When she lays down the claw.

What's the difference between a cat and a queen?
Cats have more servants.

What's it called when cats break into teams and throw poodles at each other?
Dogball.

MAX: Your kittens all look the same. How can you tell them apart?
MISTY: Well, if the mew fits...

TABBY'S TEXT MESSAGING

Fr8ee >^..^<
Fraidy cat.

K9s R A Joke
Canines are a joke.

Luv 2 Prrr
Love to purr.

Dogs R Ntz
Dogs are nuts

Katz Rok
Cats rock.

Mice R Yumy
Mice are yummy.

C@ n the H@
Cat in the Hat.

K10s Rul
Kittens rule.

F@ C@
Fat Cat.

I 1t Katz
I want cats.

8 Feline Funnies

Feline Favorites

What's a cat's favorite sports car?
  A Purrari.

What's a cat's favorite dessert?
  Chocolate mouse.

What is a cat's favorite kind of tree?
  A fur tree.

What's a cat's favorite luxury car?
A Catillac.

What's a kitten's favorite field trip?
To the mews-eum.

What's a cat's favorite movie?
Little Purr-maid.

What's the favorite Mexican food of cats?
Mice and beans.

What's a cat's favorite holiday?
Fur-th of July.

What's a cat's least favorite fish?
Dogfish.

A Breed Apart

What do you get when you cross a tailless cat with a monster?
Manxenstein.

What do you get when you cross a turtle with a feline?
A *tortoise shell cat.*

What kind of cat breed do you get when you cross a goose with a cat?
A *Honk-inese.*

How do you turn a Manx into a man?
Remove the "x".

What kind of cat runs into walls?
A *Bonkinese.*

What do you call a New England cat that acts very silly?
A *Maine Loon cat.*

CAT BREEDER: I created a new cat breed. I crossed a
    Russian Blue and a ghost.
CUSTOMER: What do you call it?
CAT BREEDER: A Russian Boo.

Purebred Knock-Knocks

Knock-knock.
  Who's there?
Abyssinian.
  Abyssinian who?
Abyssinian you later.

Knock-knock.
  Who's there?
Burmese.
  Burmese who?
Burr—mese cold out here.
Let me in!

Knock-knock.
  Who's there?
Himalayan.
  Himalayan who?
Himalayan around so much is going to get
him fired.

Wild and Crazy Relatives

Why is there a library on the savannah?
  So people can read between the lions.

What's it called when a group of small wildcats stand
arm in arm?
  A lynx-chain fence.

What kind of cat floats?
  A bobcat.

Why do lions live on the African savannah?
  Because the leopards already had the best spots.

Why was the tiger kicked out of the army?
  They found out he didn't earn his stripes.

Why did the cheetah take her cub to the eye doctor?
  He was seeing spots.

What did one leopard say to the other leopard?
  "Scratch a little higher. Ahh...that's the spot!"

What kind of dance do mountain lions do?
The puma rumba.

HALEY: Did you hear about the big cat show?
BAILEY: No, tell me about it.
HALEY: The lions were the mane event.

BOOTSY: My great-great grandfather was a famous
explorer.
MITTENS: What was his name?
BOOTSY: Pounce de Leon.

A cheetah applied for a job at an eye doctor's office.
The doctor told the cheetah that he couldn't possibly
hire him. "Why not?" asked the cheetah. The doctor
said, "I don't want my patients seeing spots before
their eyes!"

Wild & Crazy Knock-Knocks

Knock-knock.
Who's there?
Cheetah.
Cheetah who?
Cheetah's never prosper.

Knock-knock.
Who's there?
Lion.
Lion who?
Lion about your age again?

Knock-knock.
Who's there?
Ocelot.
Ocelot who?
Ocelot of pet jokes.

9 iguana Tell You a Joke

How did the snake finish his love letter?
He sealed it with a hiss.

How do lizards watch their weight?
They stand on their scales every morning.

What's it called when two lizards crash their cars?
A gecko-wrecko.

What do you get when you cross a rosebush with a bullfrog?
A thorny toad.

What do you get when you cross a small pet rodent with a man-eating sea creature?
A hamster-head shark.

Something Fishy

Where do fish eat their breakfast cereal?
In a fish bowl.

What resource do fish use for school reports?
The fin-ternet.

What kind of fish recites his ABCs while he wrestles?
An alpha-beta fighting fish.

Why did the fish want to become a lawyer?
She heard about the scales of justice.

What do tropical fish celebrate in November?
Tanks-giving.

What kind of fish has wings?
Angelfish.

What did the plain fish say to the goldfish?
"Beauty is only fin deep."

Animal Fun and Games

What's a boa constrictor's favorite game?
Twister.

What's a snail's favorite summertime toy?
Slip and slide.

What do frogs play at parties?
Leap-human.

What do mice like to play?
Hide and Go Eek.

MARY: Do you know how to make a fish dish?
ARI: Sure, just replace the "f" with a "d".

GREG: I had to put a lock on my salt-water aquarium.
MEG: Why?
GREG: I heard about a coral thief.

MATT: That snake has no sense of humor.
PAT: Why?
MATT: You can't pull his leg.

BILLY: My frog has a strange sense of humor.
MILLY: Why?
BILLY: He thinks it's funny to croak.

GREG: I made my snake shed his skin.
PEG: How did you do that?
GREG: I told him a joke that was a real side-splitter!

Two frogs hopped into a restaurant. The hostess said, "We don't serve frogs here." One frog asked, "Why not?" The hostess said, "Too many people complained they tasted like chicken."

Kooky Knock-Knocks

Knock-knock.
　　Who's there?
Answer.
　　Answer who?
Answer what my lizard eats.

Knock-knock.
　　Who's there?
Ego.
　　Ego who?
Ego pretty fast for a turtle.

Knock-Knock.
　Who's there?
Polliwogs.
　Polliwogs who?
Polliwogs a cracker.

Knock-knock.
　Who's there?
F.I. Toad.
　F.I. Toad who?
F.I. Toad you once, I
toad you a thousand
times, let me in!

Knock-knock.
　Who's there?
Python.
　Python who?
Python the windowsill
cooling.

Knock-knock.
　Who's there?
Tortoise.
　Tortoise who?
He tortoise a lie.

Knock-knock.
　Who's there?
Iguana.
　Iguana who?
Iguana hold your hand.

UNWRITTEN BOOKS

Slippery Slimy Pets by Sally Mander

Exploring the World Wide Web by Tor Ann Chula

Hissing Cousins by Rose E. Boa

Military Lizards by The Marine Iguanas

UNSUNG SONGS

"This Sand is Your Sand" by B.B. King Snake

"The Ritsy Bitsy Spider" by A. Rich Arachnid

HiLARiOUS NEWSPAPER HEADLiNES

Out of Business Sale: Fish Store Goes Belly Up

Animal Lovers Shell Out Money to Save Turtles

PET STORE TEXT MESSAGING

Cocka2s RUL
Cockatoos rule.

R@s R GR8
Rats are great.

2Mny Gupeez
Too many guppies.

How's it Going?

"It's a dog's life," said the veterinarian.

"I'm as happy as a clam," said the marine scientist.

"I'm in a blue funk," said the chameleon.

"Life stinks," said the skunk.

"I'm on cloud nine," said the angelfish.

"I'm down in the mouth," said the horse.

"Full steam ahead," said the clam.

"Just keeping my head above water," said the turtle.

"It's not what it's cracked up to be," said the chick.

"It's a small world," said the spider.

How's the Weather?

"Cloudy with a chance of reins," said the horse.

"Sunny and worm," said the frog.

"Clear and funny," said the clownfish.

"A feet-wave is upon us," said the millipede.

"Slow is in the forecast," said the tortoise.

"Sunny in spots," said the Dalmatian.

Where do furry pets go on vacation?
Club Shed.

Why was the boa constrictor in trouble?
He got himself into a tight squeeze.

Why did the python need a vacation?
He needed to unwind.

What do you get when you cross a cottontail and a frog?
A bunny ribbit.

What do you get when you cross a small vegetable and a rooster?

A peacock.

What do you get when you cross a small mammal and a fruit tree?

A guinea fig.

What do you call a sea animal that catches food with its tongue?

A clameleon.

CREEPY LiCENSE PLATES

GR8LEGS (tarantula)

FISHB8 (worms)

GMEASQZ (snake)

GIMME A SQUEEZE
FISH BAIT
GREAT LEGS

LICENSE PLATES UNLOCKED

Knock-knock.
    Who's there?
Macaw.
    Macaw who?
Macaw goes pretty fast on the highway.

Wild Guests

Knock, knock.
  Who's there?
Canary.
  Canary who?
Canary come out and play?

          Knock, knock.
            Who's there?
          Pigment.
            Pigment who?
          Pigment to say oink.

Knock, knock.
  Who's there?
Salmon.
  Salmon who?
Salmon some friends are chasing sticks.

HiLARiOUS NEWSPAPER HEADLiNES

Pet Skunk Escapes: Causes a Real Stink

Rabbit Breeder Gets Hopping Mad

10 Polly Wants a Crack-Up

What kind of birds were caught looking at each other's tests?
The para-cheats.

How do mice stay in touch with their friends?
With eek-mail.

Why do ferrets play dirty?
Because all's ferret in love and war.

What did the stuck-up weasel say to the magic mirror?

"Mirror, mirror on the wall,
Who's the ferret of them all?"

What did the farmer say when he heard his sheep talking?

"Ewe said it!"

Why did the speaker use a bale of hay for a podium?

He was a little hoarse.

Why was the hamster the star of the circus?

He put on a wheely big show.

What do you get when you cross a pumpkin and a jungle cat?
A jack-o'-leopard.

What do you get when you cross an athlete with a small parrot?
A jock-atiel.

What do you get when you cross a clownfish with a cobra?
An animal that thinks it's funny to spit.

What do you call a well-traveled animal who likes to swim?
A jet-set wet pet.

What do you get when you cross a bird, a dog, and a cow?
A cocka-poodle-moo.

What do you get when you cross a pony and a chameleon?
A horse of a different color.

What do you get when you cross a clownfish with a rabbit?
A funny bunny.

GUINEA PIG: Did you ask Gerbil if he wants to play?
CHINCHILLA: Yes, but I don't think he'll come over.
GUINEA PIG: What did he say?
CHINCHILLA: Gnaw.

What kind of desert animal hops around with a suitcase?

A pack-rabbit.

What kind of stories do rabbits like?

Cotton tales.

JUDY: Did you hear about the horse who went to school?

RUDY: No, what happened?

JUDY: He was sent to the principal's office, and the principal said, "Why the long face?"

Another horse was sent to the principal's office. The principal said, "Stop horsing around and hoof it back to class!"

Krazy Knock-Knocks

Knock-knock.
  Who's there?
Alma.
  Alma who?
Alma homework got eaten by my dog.

    Knock-knock.
      Who's there?
    Dachshund.
      Dachshund who?
    Dachshund cats make good pets.

Knock-knock.
  Who's there?
Defense.
  Defense who?
Defense is too high
for my horse to jump.

    Knock-knock.
      Who's there?
    Distinct.
      Distinct who?
    Distinct after my pet skunk got to it.

Knock-knock.
  Who's there?
Mustang.
  Mustang who?
Mustang when a bee stings you.

Early High Brow

FARMER BROWN: I've been playing a classical music CD in the hen house, and I think the rooster has been listening.

FARMER BILL: Why do you say that?

FARMER BROWN: Every morning we wake up to "Bach-a-doodle-do!"

UNSUNG SONGS

"Home Tweet Home" by I. Minnie Cage

"Baa, Baa Quack Peep" from *Farm Animal Tunes* by Cowan Pig

"Yankee Poodle" by Q.T. Pup

"Life Behind Bars" by Ginny Pig

"Jingle Smells" by S. Kunk

Polly Really Wants a Cracker

JENNY: I'll give you a cracker if you say, "debut."

POLLY: Debut is good from de mountain top.

HALEY: I'll give you a cracker if you say, "assist."

POLLY: Assist the only way I'll get a cracker?

TOMMY: I'll give you a cracker if you say, "defer."
POLLY: Defer is on de cat!

MIKE: I'll give you a cracker if you say, "catsup."
POLLY: Catsup to no good!

KATIE: I'll give you a cracker if you say, "easel."
POLLY: Easel a little stinker, isn't he?

LISA: I'll give you a cracker if you say, "account."
POLLY: Account six crackers now you all owe me!

What did one bird say to another?
Toucan live as cheaply as one.

DiD YOU HEAR THE JOKE ABOUT...

The kitten...it's a-mewsing.

The cat...it's hiss-terical!

The snake...it's a side-splitter.

The parrot...it's a scream!

The escaped zoo animals...it's a riot.

The dog who ate broccoli...it's a gas.

Silly Sayings

Polly wants a cracker...and a steak dinner with strawberry shortcake for dessert.

A bird in the hand...gets very messy.

UNWRiTTEN BOOKS

How the Finch Stole Christmas by Rob R. Byrd

Gourmet Ice Cream Recipes by Häagen Dogs

What Stray Animals Want by Ivana Holme

Knock-Knock.
Who's there?
Muumuu.
Muumuu who?
Muumuu said the cow.

Knock-knock.
Who's there?
Weasel.
Weasel who?
Weasel me a little tune.

index